Neighborhood Safari

Grasshoppers

by Dalton Rains

FOCUS READERS
PIONEER

www.focusreaders.com

Focus Readers is distributed by North Star Editions:
sales@northstareditions.com | 888-417-0195

Produced for Focus Readers by Red Line Editorial.

Photographs ©: Shutterstock Images, cover, 1, 6, 8, 10, 12, 14, 17, 18, 21; iStockphoto, 4

Library of Congress Cataloging-in-Publication Data
Names: Rains, Dalton, author.
Title: Grasshoppers / by Dalton Rains.
Description: Mendota Heights, MN: Focus Readers, [2025] | Series: Neighborhood safari | Includes bibliographical references and index. | Audience: Grades K-1
Identifiers: LCCN 2023059774 (print) | LCCN 2023059775 (ebook) | ISBN 9798889981770 (hardcover) | ISBN 9798889982333 (paperback) | ISBN 9798889983446 (pdf) | ISBN 9798889982890 (ebook)
Subjects: LCSH: Grasshoppers--Juvenile literature | Grasshoppers--Anatomy--Juvenile literature | Grasshoppers--Behavior--Juvenile literature | Grasshoppers--Life cycles--Juvenile literature
Classification: LCC QL508.A2 R35 2025 (print) | LCC QL508.A2 (ebook) | DDC 595.7/26--dc23/eng/20240125
LC record available at https://lccn.loc.gov/2023059774
LC ebook record available at https://lccn.loc.gov/2023059775

Printed in the United States of America
Mankato, MN
082024

About the Author

Dalton Rains is a writer and editor from Minnesota.

Table of Contents

Chapter 1

Jumping Away

A grasshopper rests on a warm rock. Suddenly, it sees a mouse. The mouse tries to eat the grasshopper. But the grasshopper jumps away. It lands on a nearby tree.

Grasshoppers are found in many parts of the world. They often live in areas with lots of low plants. Grasshoppers eat leaves, seeds, and flowers. They may also eat farm **crops**.

There are more than 11,000 kinds of grasshoppers.

Chapter 2

Body Parts

Grasshoppers are insects. A grasshopper's body has three parts. All grasshoppers have six legs. Most kinds also have two pairs of wings.

antennae
eye
legs
wing

A grasshopper has two **antennae** on its head. Antennae are used to touch and feel. They are also used to smell. A grasshopper has five eyes. Two eyes are large. Three eyes are small.

A grasshopper uses **mandibles** to eat.

Chapter 3

Hopping and Hiding

Grasshoppers use **camouflage**. It helps them hide from **predators**. Many grasshoppers are green or brown. They can hide near plants.

A grasshopper has large **hind** legs. These legs are strong. The grasshopper can leap to safety if it sees a predator. Sometimes the grasshopper needs to go farther. It may use its wings to fly away.

If a grasshopper is trapped, it can break off one or two legs to get away.

Swarms

Grasshoppers live alone for much of the year. Most kinds only come together to **mate**. But some grasshoppers may fly together. This is called a swarm. Swarms often form when grasshoppers need to find food.

Chapter 4

A Grasshopper's Life

Female grasshoppers lay eggs in the summer and fall. The eggs hatch in spring and early summer. Baby grasshoppers are called nymphs.

A nymph is born with no wings. It **molts** five or six times. One month after hatching, the nymph grows wings. Now it is an adult. Adult grasshoppers mate. Then, the females lay more eggs.

Adult grasshoppers live for two to three months.

Life Cycle

Female grasshoppers lay eggs in summer and fall.

Baby grasshoppers hatch in spring and early summer.

Nymphs molt up to six times.

Nymphs grow wings and become adult grasshoppers.

Adult grasshoppers mate.

FOCUS ON

Grasshoppers

Write your answers on a separate piece of paper.

1. Write a sentence describing where grasshoppers live.
2. Would you want a grasshopper to live near your home? Why or why not?
3. When do grasshopper eggs hatch?
   - A. spring and early summer
   - B. late fall and winter
   - C. late summer and fall
4. Why is it helpful for grasshoppers to be green or brown?
   - A. Those colors are easy to see.
   - B. Those colors are dark, so grasshoppers can soak up more sunlight.
   - C. Those colors blend in with plants, so predators may not see them.

Answer key on page 24.

Glossary

antenne

Long, thin body parts on an insect's head. The parts are used for sensing.

camouflage

Colors that make an animal difficult to see in the area around it.

crops

Plants that people grow to eat or sell.

hind

At the back of an animal's body.

mandibles

Jaws that stick out from an insect's head.

mate

To come together to make a baby.

molts

Loses an older covering so a new one can grow in its place.

predators

Animals that hunt other animals for food.

To Learn More

BOOKS

Garstecki, Julia. *Fast Facts About Grasshoppers.* North Mankato, MN: Capstone Press, 2021.

Schuh, Mari. *Cricket or Grasshopper?* Minneapolis: Bellwether Media, 2022.

NOTE TO EDUCATORS

Visit **www.focusreaders.com** to find lesson plans, activities, links, and other resources related to this title.

Index

Answer Key: 1. Answers will vary; **2.** Answers will vary; **3.** A; **4.** C